10 EFFECTIVE WAYS TO CHILDREN'S MINISTRY

Discover Excellent Ways To Teach Biblical Truths & Principles to Children And Young People

Lawrence E. Mukoro

SUTTON, ALASKA

All biblical references are taken from the Authorized King James Version Bible, public domain.

Copyright © 2019, Lawrence E. Mukoro

All Rights Reserved. No part of this publication may be reproduced, stored in a retrieval system or transmitted in any or by any means, electronic, mechanical, photocopy, recording or any other, except for brief quotations in printed reviews, without the prior permission of the author.

Relevant Publishers LLC
PO Box 505
Sutton, AK 99674

For More Information Please Contact:
lawrence.mukoro@yahoo.com
  Millennium Publishing
  #3, Old Warri Road, Orerokpe
  P.O. Box 1413. Effurun
  Delta State, Nigeria
  Telephone: +234 - 8136105920

10 Effective Ways to Children's Ministry: Discover Excellent Ways to Teach Biblical Truths & Principles to Children and Young People / Mukoro, Lawrence E.

ISBN: 978-3-9992605-6-2 ebook
ISBN: 978-0-9992605-7-9 print book

DEDICATION

This book is dedicated to Joy Samuel, my amazing daughter in the Lord, and every child I have ministered to while serving in Living Faith Church.

Joy, by the grace of God upon me, you are the seal of my effectiveness in children's ministry.

I love you and I'm looking forward to seeing you on the mountaintop, in the nearest future.

TABLE OF CONTENTS

Introduction 1

Chapter 1 8
Be Armed with the Word 8

Chapter 2 25
Play Like a Child, Preach Like a Pastor 25

Chapter 3 33
The Meekness Test 33

Chapter 4 43
Love Them, Hate Their Weakness 43

Chapter 5 50
Be A Cheerful Giver 50

Chapter 6 57
Build Family Relationships 57

Chapter 7 63
Practice Patience Beyond Limits 63

Chapter 8 68
Be Their Intercessor 68

Chapter 9 74
Embrace All Children 74

Chapter 10 79
Catch a Personal Vision for Them 79

Epilogue 89

FOREWORD

When I was first asked to read Pastor Lawrence Mukoro's new book, *10 Effective Ways to Children's Ministry: Discover Excellent Ways To Teach Biblical Truths & Principles to Children And Young People*, I was a little nervous because I did not specialize in Children's Ministry and had spent the majority of my ministry time teaching adults, with the rare exceptions of working in Children's Church as a substitute teacher. However, by the end of the first chapter, I realized Pastor Lawrence's book was applicable to all ministries. These principles are timeless and very accurate to even those working in adult ministries.

Whether or not you're currently deployed on the mission field of formal children's ministry, this book provides deep insight to understanding the value of raising up the next generation for Christ and details practical insights on how to make that happen. Pastor Lawrence has really discovered effective ways to minister to children through the insight of the Holy Spirit and Scriptures and his time working with children. The lessons he shares in his new book will benefit your own children, grandchildren, nieces and nephews, as well as all the other children you meet in church. Wherever we go in life, there are children ready and willing to hear the Word of God if we will simply reach out to them.

If you've ever avoided Children's Ministry in the past, Pastor Lawrence will ignite a holy fire and awaken a desire within your heart to reach the Future Church. Those new to Children's Ministry or who have been looking to gain practical knowledge on how to become more effective for the Kingdom of God with the children in their care will be blessed to find deep insight and practical steps to apply. One of the most valuable lessons **10 Effective Ways to Children's Ministry** provides is the importance of growing your relationship with Christ and the Word in every area of ministry, especially children's ministry.

In these ten short chapters, I gleaned more understanding of how to reach children for the glory of Jesus Christ than I had ever been exposed to in church over the last fifteen years. I loved Pastor Lawrence's statement, "The future of the church of Jesus Christ of tomorrow is revealed in our children today." **Our children are the future of the Church!** Every minister who wants to be successful for God should never neglect this simple fact and needs the skills in this book to evangelize to every person in every season.

Sharon Aubrey,
Author of Jesus Unveiled

INTRODUCTION

Whether you are called specifically to minister to children in the church, are an adult with an undying love for children, or you are a stay at home parent, whose desire is to instill the fear of the Lord in your children, this book is for you. *10 Effective Ways to Children's Ministry: Discover Excellent Ways To Teach Biblical Truths & Principles to Children And Young People* will give you a new perspective, provide insight, resources and wisdom on how to love and teach children in the ways of the Lord.

This book will reveal the unique role of children in Christian ministry and explain how to effectively teach Sunday school by involving children in church leadership and including them in the decision making process for church growth and ultimately the growth of the Kingdom of God. Before assuming my current pastorate in Millennium Christian Church, I served as a children's minister with Living Faith Church, Nigeria for seven years. During this period I was privileged to be an active children's minister in four different local assemblies of the Church. Even though my employment took me throughout Nigeria, I was still able to continue to serve in children's ministry during these times and stages of my life throughout many different places. This widened my experience considerably in this area.

In all four local assemblies within this seven-year period, the ministerial leaders I worked with saw the good fruit of my labor. They recognized my abilities and gifts to have an effective and efficient children's ministry. Admittedly, I knew this in part within myself and being around children has always doubled my joy. My experience, passion, and desires stood out in one of the local assemblies, where I was elected to serve as one of the children's church ministry leaders for two years.

My heart for children and children's ministry was the first door God opened for me in ministry. His plans and purposes and the fullness of them are continuing to be expanded in my life. "No calling in the kingdom of God is higher than another.

"No calling in the kingdom of God is higher than another.

Before I began children's ministry, God had already unveiled His plans and purposes for my life. He has used the children ministry as a preparatory platform for me. Children's ministry was my first place of training, pruning, and proper grooming for the full time ministry I am in today as the pastor of Millennium Christian Church. The Holy Spirit solely led me to this ministry in January 2009, and by this, a little practice here, a little practice there, I mastered the ability of preaching from a pulpit. Today, I'm comfortable and happy preaching, to God alone be given all the glory.

Although I experienced good success in advancing God's kingdom within the children's ministry, I was never ignorant to the truth behind my effectiveness, voiced by the Apostle Paul in **1 Corinthians 15:10,**

"But by the grace of God I am what I am: and his grace which bestowed upon me was not in vain; but I labored more abundantly than they all: yet not I, but the grace of God which was with me."

I made full proof of my children's ministry and apparently my success appeared to all around, but I knew quiet clearly, it was not me but an inner force driving me to work. I was being empowered by the Holy Spirit to produce desirable results both spiritually and intellectually in the lives of the children and the entire children chapels.

To be an effective children's minister is to make full proof of your ministry before God and man. The workings of our success being revealed before heaven and earth, clearly demonstrates this is impossible on a human level. That is, we know every divine mission requires divine support. The apostles tarried in the upper house until they were empowered by the Holy Spirit. That same day Peter preached and about three thousand people surrendered to the Lord Jesus. This was the beginning of their effect in Jerusalem and beyond.

Again, to be effective is to produce desirable results and of course no man has the capacity to produce any kind of results in God's kingdom except when the Holy Spirit works through them. It is the Holy Spirit's ministry to empower you to be effective as you serve in God's Kingdom. This is one of His chief ministries on the earth today. He is looking out for the vessels that are due for empowerment and empowering them. Empowerment by the Holy Spirit makes you effective in any aspect of ministry work. Many desire to be effective and even more effective in what they are doing for the Lord today, even those in the secular world. It is a natural appetite for the average person to seek to continue to improve and grow in all they do.

What ministry are you effective in? Effectiveness comes in degrees, just as empowerment is given in degrees. Seemingly, none of us have the prize yet, and we won't until the Lord gives us the crown of life. However, we must all be determine like the apostle Paul said in **Philippians 3: 12-14,**

> **"Not as though I had already attained, ether were already perfect: but I follow after, if that I may apprehend that for which also I am apprehended of Christ Jesus. Brethren, I count not myself to have apprehended: but this one thing I do, forgetting those things which are behind, and reaching forth unto those things which are before, I press toward the mark for the prize of the high calling of God in Christ Jesus."**

My friend, let this same mind be in you that was also in this beloved apostle, no matter what we do for God we should count not ourselves to have attained it yet.

It saddens me that I didn't utilize all the time and gifts God provided to me in my beginning in children's ministry. I did not wholly realize the value of what I had been given. Now my excitement grows, because I am pouring out upon all the children God is bringing to us at Millennium Christian Church. It's a good thing we all have a natural appetite for effectiveness. Maturity dictates that some of us are more thirsty and hungry for it than others. All in all, none of us are walking alone.

We all have the power to be effective in what we do for God. Therefore, to be effective is not human thing to achieved but the Spirit of God walking with us and until we yield ourselves to Him. I mean you need to surrender, submit, and give in to the Holy Spirit. There is little or nothing you can do — this is not a kingdom of effort for by strength shall no man prevail.

However, let's not be deceived in the kingdom of God there are promises, principles, demands and commands. Often times we love the promises without following the principles. We want the supplies without meeting the demands and the commands are considered too difficult for us to keep. In God's kingdom there are principles and certain principles contain certain promises. In my research I gathered the definitions of principles and demands from the Microsoft Encarta Dictionary. Principles are simply "ethical standards or basic ways in which something works." Demands means "a forceful request; a clear and firm request that is difficult to ignore or deny."

A team player in a football game might play on the field and later be called out to sit on the bench, being reserved for a more crucial game ahead. In this same way I now have broader view from personal experience. I am like this team player watching other effective players playing in the field. I have noticed something both in me and other effective ministers as I have watched from inside and outside the game. The same principles and demands are working for all of us.

What is most important for you understand is the Holy Spirit is the dynamos power that can come upon any vessel to deliver maximally God's will in all fields of ministry. His principles and commandments are same in every nation and land. God is no respecter of persons. If you meet his commandments or demands, you have therefore made yourself visible to Him to work in your life. It's just like when you follow the principles of science you expect the results for surety. For instance, the Scripture tells us it is grace that brings salvation and this grace has appeared to all men (*See* Titus 2:11). But not all men are saved today. Yet, this is a promise from Father God. The principle of salvation says he who believes in his heart that Jesus Christ is the Son of God and confess with his mouth shall be saved. (*See* Romans 10:9-10). It therefore means if I believe but never confess that Jesus Christ is the Son of God, my Lord, I am still not saved. The Holy Spirit is the embodiment of power for all children of God for effective works, but are all believers effective in their works? I leave that to you to ponder.

God is no respecter of persons.

But then, how do I combat this lack of knowledge of those who do not understand these principles? By God's grace, I am well pleased to share all of my successes and experience utilizing these principles. Whether on the field or off the field, if you are willing, follow me, I along with the Holy Spirit will teach you, how to be part of an effective children's ministry.

You will be marked by Heaven and earth as a key player in children's ministry, as I unveil these salient principles to you. But most importantly, these principles and demands do not work for readers but only for doers. I love how the apostle James put it,

> "But be doers of the word, and not hearers only, deceiving your own selves. For he beholdeth himself, and goeth his way, and straightway forgetteth what manner of man he was. But whoso looketh into the perfect law of liberty, and continueth therein, he being not a forgetful hearer, but a doer of the work, this man shall be <u>BLESSED</u> in his deeds."
> James 1:22-25

Maybe you should circle the word *blessed* in your Bible and to think of it additionally as the word *effective*. This will give a more powerful meaning to what you have just read relatively to our context here.

Finally, my friend let's get started!

Chapter One

Be Armed With the Word

"For the word of God is quick, and powerful, and sharper than any two-edged sword, piercing even to the dividing asunder of soul and spirit, and of the joints and marrow, and is a discerner of the thoughts and intents of the heart."
Hebrews 4:12

**"Nobody ever outgrows Scripture;
the book widens and deepens with our years"
—Charles H. Spurgeon**

As bow and arrows are weapons in the hands of a warrior so is the Word a weapon in the minister's heart and mouth. No one makes it into God's kingdom without the Word in your heart and mouth. The Word keeps us from falling short of His glory, as well as it gives us victory over the enemy at anytime and any day. Like in the days of Adam and in the time of Christ Jesus, the same old serpent showed up with the same old tricks in Genesis and Matthew. Christ Jesus received the victory because He used the Word to overcome the enemy where Adam did not. In fact, the Son is the Word himself. No one can defeat Him.

A children's minister is like every a captain who stands to prepare and organize his troops for battle. The captain doesn't just prepare and deploy troops; he trains his troops in weapons and instruments of war. As a children's minister, this is what you have been called out to do for the children. Prepare and train them with the Word, and when it is time, deploy them also through the Word. You see, this is so important. It is why we need to put on the whole armor of God so that we may be able to stand against the wiles of the enemy. We need to especially understand the Word of God and the victory it contains, for every other weapon is wrapped up in it.

NOVICE IN THE WORD

As many that are led by the Spirit of God to serve as ministers in the children's ministry, whether be novice or not, welcome them all, and cast no one away as the Lord Jesus Christ said of Himself (*See* John 6:37). The entrance level doesn't matter provided they are led by Him and have a willing heart to truly serve God's purpose at that time of their life. But to remain a novice in the Word should be highly discouraged by the children's ministry leadership. As a believer whether newborn or not, we are to daily feed on the Word of God for spiritual growth and perfection. How much more is required of those who represent the church in ministry.

> **"As newborn babes, desire the sincere milk of the word, that you may grow thereby:"**
> **1 Peter 2:2**

Ministry workers who are *novice* in the Word should desire the sincere milk of the Word like other believers for their spiritual growth. Is that not the purpose of the

Bible as stated in 2 Timothy 3:17, **"That the man of God may be perfect, thoroughly furnished unto all good works."** The room for improvement should be limitless, therefore personally improve your word level for the office you are holding, and in so doing, you are not just growing thereby but also arming yourself fully for your job in a children's ministry.

Personally improve your "Word" level for the office you are holding.

In my experience, I have seen ministers who read our teaching outlines and still couldn't impart the children with the message in it. Likewise, I've also seen the ones who never made it to attend the teaching preview, skimming the teaching outline and yet made a very tremendous impact without deviating from the original intent of the message. The difference between these two groups is the amount of the Word they have ingested over time. Whoever has the Word in their mind and hearts, the Holy Spirit is able to use and pour out the Word through them to others. This is it! The benefit of feeding on the Word is not just to grow and mature spiritually, but it is a source of influence for the Holy Spirit for impactful teachings and ministrations. In any case, it's a simultaneous effect.

FIRST PRINCIPLES OF THE ORACLES OF GOD

"For when for the time ye ought to be teachers, ye have need that one teach you again which is the first principles of the oracles of God; and are become such as have need of milk, not of strong meat."
Hebrews 5:12

The Lord gives the body of Christ gifts by the Holy Spirit, of knowledge, wisdom, discernment and understanding and many other gifts, regardless of age to teach His people. Kids and teens are inclusive in God's people, in fact very special people as the Lord Jesus Christ said of them: **"Except ye be converted, and become as little children, ye shall not enter into the kingdom of heaven."** (Matthew 18:3). Every child of God is anointed of God, men and women whom through God teaches His children (old and young) knowledge, wisdom, and understanding of His kingdom. Maybe you are a stay-at-home mom or a busy dad who still finds quality time to teach your children about God. I personally identify you as a lay minister. It matters not the type of minister you are before God and man. **The first rule for you as a minister is that you become a student first,** though matured, but become in your heart a person that has need for milk and not of strong meat. It is needful for you to have a teacher for you yourself to learn from. This may be the pastor of your church or any other mentor the Lord has led you to.

"Learners learn with the attitude of humility: there is so much more for me to know"
– Brian C. Stiller

To cultivate a learner's mentality, you require teachers from whom you learn to have sound doctrines and the Word of God. Like Timothy, you must have a Paul from whom you will be mentored on an ongoing basis.

A children's minister will be most effective if first they covet a passion to learn. Any lacking in this gift should make a request to God for it. It is in this humble spirit that makes you regularly desire to improve upon yourself and become excellent in all you do for God in His kingdom.

In contrast, the Holy Spirit is the greatest teacher anyone can ever have in God's kingdom, He is our Helper. He is always there to lead us into all truth, and He does speak Himself, for as He hears from the Lord He speaks to us. The Holy Spirit is dynamic in His ways and knows more than what you and all your earthly teachers put together know. The Holy Spirit knows the spiritual needs of His children, even those you find difficult and unsaved in your church. He will instruct you on how to minister to them. His knowledge and revelations are always current and relevant that we may experience triumphant ministries today. You need to partner and embrace His ministry warmly. Following His lead, you will find ease in serving children in more excellent and effective ways, in the church, home, or the market place. Quick obedience is a requirement on your part to enhance the teaching ministry of the Holy Spirit.

"I have yet many things to say unto you, but ye cannot bear them now. Howbeit when he, the Spirit of truth, is come, he will guide you into all truth: for he shall not speak of himself; but whatever he shall hear, that shall he speak: and he will shew you things to come."
John 16:12-13

There are many things the Lord Jesus wants to reveal to us from a child's perspective about His kingdom. If we provoke our children to wrath (Ephesians 6:4), not only will our children miss out on important instruction, but so will we. When the Holy Spirit takes these things from the Lord and reveals them to you, it becomes simple to understand them. His teaching ministry makes wise the simple, its light breaks obscurity of all kinds. With the Holy Spirit, you are sure to be instant with the Word in season and out of season. Choose your battles with your children, but bring them up in the nurture and admonition of the Lord. This way you will always be prepared to give a word.

He knows what you do not know and receives what you do not have the capacity to receive and breaks it down bit-by-bit for your maximum understanding. As you begin to listen and carry out His teachings, relating heart-to-heart daily with Him, you will begin to notice steady progress in your ministry. Many around you will begin to see the glory of God operating in your ministry sooner than you know it.

THE FUTURE CHURCH

The future of the church of Christ of tomorrow is revealed in our children today. In other words the children **are** the future of the church of Christ. If you want to build a successful ministry, it will require a counting of costs and adequate preparations to achieve it. This means, if the Lord Jesus Christ tarries in His coming, the church of tomorrow will be presided by the children of today. Imagine that! These children can be the next evangelists, pastors, prophets, teachers and apostles in our churches, in our homes and communities. The men and women who will take over church leadership tomorrow and plant new ministries across the globe are our own children today. Isn't this a WOW factor?

This is why it is so important the kind of doctrines they receive today. It is a great concern of mine. Children should not have false teachers, who are twisting the Word of God, and indoctrinating them with devils' doctrines. This should be a concern of yours too, especially in this fallen world where Christian nations are becoming godless and carnality is on the increase. It grieves my heart when I ponder on the kind of world innocent children will have to live in, in the future.

This is my inspiration and the essence of this book to help ministry workers discover the excellent ways to teach our church children. We need to do this job effectively not just for our future but also for theirs and the many others that will learn from them.

Will the church of tomorrow be of the Holy Ghost and living for Christ or some other god? We determine this today by how our children's ministers allow themselves to be influenced by the Holy Spirit.

Our children today will be church leadership tomorrow.

THE CHILD TIMOTHY

Timothy knew the Holy Scriptures right from his childhood (2 Timothy 3:15). This was possible with the help of his teachers, his Grandmother Lois, his Mother Eunice (2 Timothy 1:5), and the Apostle Paul, his beloved father in the Lord. The fruit of these effective teachers was evidenced in the church at Ephesus, which was committed to him. He made a full proof it and other missionary walks he took with his master Paul. The role of children's teachers cannot be over emphasized as well as the role of effective teachers cannot be underestimated. Teachers in general play a larger role in nation building than most realize, they hold a position of influence both at Church and in regular school. Ministry and public leaders should know that, **'what a parent is to a child at home is what a teacher is to a child in Church and School.'** They are very influential in children's development. The bottom line is that children's ministries should be highly integrated to build a sustainable spiritual church for Christ. On the contrary are the sons of Eli, the prophet of Israel, they were supposed to inherit the priesthood of Israel in the second generation and have it forever (See 2 Samuel 27-30). Due to the lack of the Holy Scripture in them they missed a generational blessing and incurred upon their lineage a generational curse instead, from making the Lord's people to transgress and abusing the tabernacle of God. In Psalms 119:9 and 11, it states how the Word will empower any believer over sin and all unrighteous living. Apparently, the sons of Eli, Hophni and Phinehas, had not hid the word in their heart; for if they had, they wouldn't have lost such generational blessings God had predestined for their family.

We cannot afford to twist our words here. Eli did not effectively prepare the boys for the future as Lois, Eunice and Paul did with Timothy as he was growing up. We can affirm this in the Scripture.

> **"For I have told him that I will judge his house for ever for the iniquity which he knoweth because his sons made themselves vile, and he restrained them not. And therefore I have sworn unto the house of Eli, that the iniquity of Eli's house shall not be purged with sacrifice nor offering for ever."**
> **1 Samuel 3:13-14**

Do you see this? This was not for something Eli did but for something he failed to do. He failed as a parent to caution his children and raise them according to the Lord's standards. Amazingly, when I first read this, I read it as **"for the iniquity he know not"** because I first read Chapter 2: 24-25:

"Nay, my sons; for it is no good report that I hear: ye make the LORD'S people to transgress. If one man sin against another, the judge shall judge him: but if a man sin against the LORD, who shall intreat for him? Notwithstanding they hearkened not unto the voice of their father, because the LORD would slay them."

Then the Holy Spirit prompted me to reread Chapter 3 verses 13 again: When I did, I wept knowing that before Eli was advising his sons, God had already purposed in His heart to do what He will do. This means, Eli knew earlier but didn't move quickly to rebuke his sons. Eli was too late rebuking them. God had already said he would slay them, because they listened to him not. They were in rebellion. The just Judge had already judged their case and gave a verdict unknown to Eli.

Teachers, parents and guardians must be prompt to rebuke their children from every act of unrighteousness, from the time they become aware of it. This was Eli's punishment. It is an example for us for correction both to ministers, parents and guardians. Come to think of it, the punishment would have been avoided had Eli really raised his sons with the fear of the Lord by putting the Holy Scriptures in their hearts, beginning in childhood like the example used with Timothy.

The question to you as a minister, and moms and dads, are you an Eli or a Paul? Don't get me wrong. This is not to undermine the great service of the servant of God both to the people of Israel and to God Himself. All I am saying here is that despite our great works we are all doing for God today, we must ensure one of our top priorities is in teaching the future generations, specifically the future church should the Lord tarry.

Never underestimate the power of intercessory prayer.

While serving at Living Faith Church alongside other great children's teachers and with the help of the Holy Spirit, we shared the knowledge of the Lord with the children He brought across our paths. After I left those cities, on occasion I have checked back to see how the children were doing. I later found out how worldly some of those young ones had become as they grew up. I felt bad at hearing this news. The Holy Spirit reminded me in these sad moments that **consistency** is the key. We must keep teaching and mentoring these children as they grow into teens and full adults. We should consider helping them to identify their true calling in God's kingdom irrespective of the distance or other issues that may poise to us. We thank God for the positive tools of the Internet and social media. These can be very effective communication and teaching tools with those that are separated from us by reason of distance. Nevertheless, I still create opportunities to visit such towns whenever I can. During my visits I will check in with them to pray and provide counseling in their homes, even sharing to include their parents if they are home too. This is another way to build family friendships. I will be expanding on the importance of **family friendships** later in this book.

I maintain contact with children and parents wherever possible using the telephone, emails and social media. All in all, the Lord continues to bring their names to my heart and mind in my daily prayers, especially those I may not be able to see soon. I thank Father God and give Him all the glory for His sufficient grace upon me to continually hold these precious boys and girls in my prayers. My friend, never underestimate the power of intercessory prayer, it effects are far reaching, and prayer has no borders.

LABOUR IN THE WORD AS A MINISTER

> "Study to shew thyself approved unto God, a workman that needeth not be ashamed, rightly dividing the word of truth."
> 2 Timothy 2:15

The time you spent in the Word and the effort put into your searching these Scriptures is never wasted. Certainly, it will produce good fruits from the lives of the children you minister to and as well in your own life. The Word of God gives us divine knowledge, which carries transformative power both for ourselves and those we minister the Word to. To labor in the Word placed the minister at a vantage position whereby he may influence the children positively for Christ Jesus. Regrettably, many children's ministers do not search and meditate the Scriptures even though they may love to teach. They have a wrong perspective of the assignment they are doing in God's kingdom. They enjoy the exercise of teaching children but have not prepared their minds and hearts in the Scriptures. We are to be ready in season and out of season (2 Timothy 4:2). We will dig deeper into this in the next chapter.

When it comes to the Word, we have seen many teachers that are weak and lazy when it comes to their own to studies. Amazingly, some are always asking God for more grace to study the Word and yet never taking responsibility. They are expecting God to download the entire Bible in their head. Well, this will not still profit you anything, because a Bible in your head will only be knowledge.

You can still lack discernment and understanding for applying these Bible Scriptures demonstrating wisdom in your day-to-day lives. But those of you who have thoroughly meditated on these Scriptures, hiding them in your heart, you will be empowered and the children you teach will be transformed. (Psalm 1:1-6).
Howbeit, teachers who truly labor in the Word with much time and effort produce results that speak out volumes in their ministry; transforming the children, the general church and with great benefits in their life as seen in **2 Timothy 5:17:**

> **"Let the elders that rule well be counted of double honor, especially they who labor in the word and doctrine."**

As a children's pastor you are held to the same standards as the lead pastor of the local church. You are also required to create personal Bible study time, morning devotions, etc., if you are expecting to have the results with children as the lead pastors do with adults.

Corporate Bible study is a start in your preparation, but won't be sufficient to complete your tasks. Your personal one-on-one communion with the author of the Word will revive you with an excitement for effective children's ministry. You never know the plan God has for your future. He may be preparing you to become a parish pastor, deacon or some other ministry leader, and you needed experience in children's church as a preparatory platform. God is a master planner. He knows why you are, where you are, and who you are. You never know what He has up His sleeve, except you are in His plan.

Remember, working in the children's ministry could be a launch pad for you into larger ministry opportunities, part of His perfect plan and will be just like it was for me. This kind of experience cannot be obtained from any seminary or theology college around the globe. Be diligent with what you are doing for Him today, and He will surely bring you before kings.

USE THE WORD TO MINISTER

> "How forcible are right words! But what doth your arguing reprove?"
> Job 6:25

Our life experiences and stories with that of other people we have read and heard of, are wonderful and plausible when we share them with the Word during teaching periods. However they can never be compared relatively to the penetrative and transformative power of the Word of God. As we see in Hebrews 4:12 the Word is indeed penetrative and transformative:

> **"For the word of God is quick, and powerful, and sharper than any two edged sword, piercing even to the diving asunder of soul and spirit, and of the joints and marrow, and is a discerner of the thoughts and intents of the heart."**

The word of God is sharper than any electromagnetic rays you can think of. It will penetrate both the soft and hard spot of any child or adult, which will in turn lead to salvation and new life in Christ Jesus. Samuel never knew the Lord because the Word of the Lord was not yet revealed to Him. We can see that in 1 Samuel 3:7:

> **"Now Samuel did not yet know the LORD, neither was the word of the LORD yet revealed unto him."**

But in verses 21, the Scripture says:

> **"...for the LORD revealed himself to Samuel in Shiloh by the word of the LORD."**

The Word is so important, for it is the foundation of Christianity. This book is reflective of my understanding of the principles found in the Word of God as revealed to me by the Holy Spirit. The Lord will reveal himself to the children you are teaching through His Word spoken by your mouth. Let His Word confirm His creation that they may see all around them the demonstrated Glory of the Lord in their lives today. (Psalm 19:1-4). Your own stories may be good and plausible, all the same let His Word become foremost in your mouth. Break it down for the children into bite size pieces, allowing the Holy Spirit to do the impartation.

At this point, I want to acknowledge the ministry where I served as a children's minister. The Word was a priority in all their teaching outlines. Lessons were usually prepared by a small group of people respected by the leadership to be filled in the Word. This group was referred to as *Word Arm*. In three out of the four local assemblies I ministered in, myself and others worked actively in the *Word Arm* group preparing the teaching outline for the month. It was then brought before the other teachers for review.

At other times, I personally completed the teaching outlines for each month and brought them before all teachers for review for the month. I had opportunity to do this on several occasions and I'm excited to report that the time and effort I spent has helped to train and prepare me for where I am today. As much as the church places importance on this preparation strategy, not all ministers in that ministry follow through. Some never show up for the review meetings nor find personal time to review those lessons and the Scriptures in them. Although this is a good strategy and highly recommended that all ministries should adopt this method, the children's church leadership must be diligent in following up on the teachers, ensuring teachers are indeed using the Scriptures in their class outlines. Never expect people to give you what they themselves do not have. Where are they going to teach from if they themselves have not been filled in the first place?

For those of you in ministry make the effort, go for the Word. By doing so, you will be preserving the future church and simultaneously bringing honor and blessing to your own life and ministry. (Luke 11:28). The Word is fire, and it burns away any chaff in the life of the children. It is like hammer breaking every hard and difficult child. When used to minister the Word is the demonstration of God's power that changes hearts. Man's wisdom does not lead to any good manifestations in our lives.

Never expect people to give you what they themselves do not have.

Chapter Two

Play Like a Child Preach Like a Pastor

"And the streets of the city shall be full of boys and girls playing in the streets thereof."
Zechariah 8:5

**"Efficiency is doing things right;
Effectiveness is doing the right things"**
—Peter Drucker

We must all understand that children generally love playing of any kind. It's their makeup and they love whoever will come down low and play with them. Basically, you should be able to have some great fun with them and still not lose control of your class in the children's church. Is it difficult? Yes, it can be difficult. That is the fine line that can make the difference between being effective and being ineffective; whether you become efficient and over the top, or under the bar.

By nature, I am a disciplinarian. My parents, siblings, wife and every child I have ministered to and colleagues I have worked alongside of will attest to this truth. And yet again, children will flock all around me wherever I minister. I recall mentioning to a prayer partner, that wherever I walk I must carry invisible children around me that attract the children to me. If anyone desires a child especially for believing parents, I sense an anointing by grace, to encourage them for children as they desire. I believe I have this anointing of God upon my life. I have had some cases in the past when I sense the Holy Spirit reveal to tell some expectant mothers that either they were pregnant or He is going to visit them soon in answer to their prayers. One of these testimonies includes that of my prayer partner and also my younger sister who had believed God for a male child and received the same. To God alone I give all the glory for these miracles! I carry a love and a compassion for children gifted from God.

Children by nature are attracted to play and anything that may amuse them along with games of all kinds. The children will also be attracted to any adult who has interests along this line.

Some adults are only playful and never get teach the Word to the children. Some are so serious minded that the children avoid being around them as the focus is all on studies. In Africa, there is an adage that says, "**When you use one hand to beat a child, you use the other hand to draw him back**". The mystery revealed in this adage is, God gave us two hands, figuratively, one to discipline and the other to love and play. You must teach the Word and establish play times in equal amounts or you will not be successful in ministry with the children or their parents or guardians.

This alone is the main difference between children's ministry and a pastor who preaches to adults. The pastor does not play with anyone while preaching to adults and generally preaches the undiluted Word of God. It is assumed everyone called as an adult has overcome childishness and is now serious and somewhat focused requiring to be fed meat. If you do not play well or like playing, it is can be very difficult to minister to children compared to other ministry groups.

Children by nature are attracted to play.

Recently, one of the kids from the previous church with whom I had built good family ties with her, her parents and siblings phoned me. I put the phone on loudspeaker so my wife could hear too. She was busy talking and reporting everyone's misdemeanors to me thereby not giving me the chance to even get a word in edgewise. Rather I was just saying Okay! Yes! Alright! My wife kept laughing and laughing all through the remaining evening, because Joy was doing all the talking, she was so excited to be speaking with me, a thousand miles away. She is a child after my own heart, but one who I don't even know when I will be able to get to see in the near future. Yet she desires to maintain this wonderful connection. This same child who enjoys my fellowship also cries and repents of wrong deeds when my mouth moves my right hand. Using the Word as my rod is so effective that all the children around me feel the pain when I discipline another with the Word.

SINGING, JUMPING, DANCING, SHOUTING, RHYMING...

These activities and many more are part of the greater fun for children and ministers alike in the children's church. Effective ministers should not be allergic to any activities even if they don't enjoy them personally. They should not give the children any kind of a negative impression or an excuse not to participate in play. Remember the Scripture says:

> "I can do all things through Christ which strengtheneth me."
> **Philippians 4: 13**

Have a *'can do'* mentality. If you believe you can eventually you will be able *'to do.'* The problem is, most wants to be perfect in their own eyes first, but it doesn't work that way. Practice makes perfect. This is where you can win the children's hearts. When you begin to share the light in God's Word, in truth and actions, their hearts will melt and expand. Where they need repentance and growth, they will grow because someone is reaching them on all levels through the Word of God. This is what I refer to as the 360 degree ministry—it continues to go around and around continuously.

Young children who are allowed to be children are very energetic and vibrant at this stage of their lives, unlike many of us adults. They are ready to go miles past our abilities in these physical aspects of games and play. But remember, the Word of the Lord Jesus Christ does say, anyone who compels you to go one mile, go with him two. Chuckling! In any case, care should be taken with teachers who are pregnant and they should be exempted from some of the more difficult activities. But for the rest of you, have no excuse. Do not just sit back there as the coach, roll up your sleeves and join in with the players. It's great fun! You may even get a good workout out of it.

> "For bodily exercise profiteth little..."
> 1 Timothy 4:8

Yes, it profits little and in this context, little is something. Don't you think so too? Effective leaders are in agreement with me for sure on this one.

TRUST YOUR SPIRIT TO DISCERN THE TIMING

> "There is an appointed time for everything. And there is a time for every event under heaven, A time to give birth and a time to die; A time to plant and a time to uproot what is planted. A time to weep and a time to LAUGH: A time to mourn and a time to DANCE A time to throw stones and a time to gather stones; A time EMBRACE and a time to SHUN EMBRACING A time to search and a time to give up as lost; A time to keep and a time to throw away. A time to tear apart and a time to sew together; A time to be SILENT and a time to SPEAK. A time to LOVE and a time to hate (Discipline); A time for war and a time for peace."
> (Emphasis mine)
> **Ecclesiastes 3:1–8**

Time is a common determinant factor in knowing when to play and when to teach or preach. Especially when dealing with difficult and unsaved children, you don't determine the time, the Holy Spirit does. This is why it is pivotal for a minister to be spiritually sensitive when responding with kids who may be hypersensitive in a controlling atmosphere in the church class. A lot of things can happen especially with these types of children in your class. There are times when you feel like disciplining a child but the Holy Spirit will breathe a cool warning into your system. If you ignore His signal or are not aware of it, it may lead to a difficult situation with that child and also with your class. Especially in regards to discipline, we must observe the right time to action. Scripture provides a warning against provoking the child.

> "Fathers, provoke not your children to anger, lest they be discouraged."
> Colossians 3:21

A right word from us but at the wrong time may discourage our children from learning a timely lesson; far worse it may cause children to withdraw from us in the church and at home.

There are times when evil can occupy a child's heart, and effective ministers will switch to love to rebuke the enemy in the child's heart. Love conquers all including the devil. Use discernment to decide when to switch your right hand for the left hand.

Be Instant In Season And Out Of Season

> "*Preach the word; be instant (ready) in season, out of season; reprove, rebuke, exhort with all longsuffering and doctrine. For the time will come when they will not endure sound doctrine; but after their own lusts shall they heap (chose) to themselves teachers, having itching ears; And they shall turn away their ears from the truth, and shall be turned unto fables."*
> 2 Timothy 4:2-4

Effective ministers are teachers whom are ready with the Word at all times whether in times of playing or preaching. The Word for the moment is always on their tongue. This is the in season and out of season. Someone reading this book might be saying in their heart this Scripture is not applied to children. Well, you are wrong because no part of this Scripture is of private interpretation as we saw in 2 Peter 1:20. That connotes the Scripture is for all people groups.

> **"For time will come when they will not endure sound doctrine, but after their own lusts shall they heap to themselves teachers, having itching ears."**

Perhaps you are not aware let me shock you a little. Did you know that children and teens now select the teachers or classes that they like to attend? This way they can avoid the reprove and rebuke of a teacher who is actually setting them on the right path through the Word.

This is what I call selective learning. Unfortunately some parents subscribe to this rebellious behavior by calling on the children's church leadership to change their children to other classes. Parents and guardians even go so far as having shouting matches challenging the minister, not unlike undisciplined parents in the regular school system.

Even in a playing season be prepared with the Word. The difference here is that being an effective minister you will know when to use the right word in all seasons. When you yourselves are seasoned men and women who have eaten the Word, these same words will flow out of your mouths easily when needed. You will know the right word to rebuke, reprove, admonish and edify. Do not be like those desiring to be teachers, yet having no understanding of the Word as it is written. (1Timothy 1: 7).

Even in a playing season be prepared with the Word.

Chapter Three

The Meekness Test

"Whosoever therefore shall humble himself as this little child, the same is the greatest in the kingdom of heaven."
Matthew 18:4

"A proud man is always looking down on things and people; and, of course, as long as you're looking down, you can't see something that's above you."
— C.S. Lewis

The meekness test is what I refer to as the ultimate entry test. You must pass this test for to be certified to enter into a children's world as an effective minister.

MEEKNESS

As I'm pondering over this word during the wee hour of the day at my devotional study the Holy Spirit impressed in my heart these words, 'your meekness will be tested when you are with people who don't value your humility.' I hope this statement will become clearer to you later. An example of this is when you find yourself in an environment that requires you to learn from your students while you are supposed to be the one teaching.

I termed it 'The Ultimate Entry Test' because nobody who wants to be effective should teach children or think of teaching children if they lack meekness. I can guarantee you, without meekness the result will be certain—you will quickly use the exit door.

THE WAYS OF GOD ARE NOT THE WAYS OF MAN

Apparently, no one can ever succeed as a children teacher if he or she is not meek. To be meek is not only to be mild and quiet, also it is to be teachable and been ready to learn from those that you even teach. This is the way of God. We cannot know whom or what God will use to teach us. We must give room to hear even a child's opinion. You will be surprised and shocked about what they know and the depth of their understanding of a subject. Kids have given me many clever and insightful definitions that I have recorded in my journal for future review and encouragement.

Learn wisdom from the mouths of children.

These are the kinds of things that will set you apart from other ministers as EFFECTIVE from those who carry too much pride. Perhaps you are considering joining the children's ministry. I can assure you, when you start this journey you will know you can learn wisdom from the mouths of children—but it require meekness on your part to accept this truth, some children have more understanding than their teachers just like David said in **Psalm 119:99;**

> "I have more understanding than all my teachers…"

Usually teachers like to take pride in their job, that is okay officially but accept the reality of this truth. The Spirit of Wisdom can come on anyone regardless of age. There is an account of King Josiah in the scripture:

> **"Josiah was eight years old when he began to reign and he reigned thirty and one years in Jerusalem… And he did that which was right in the sight of the LORD, and walked in all the way of David his father, and turned not aside to the right or to the left."**
> **2 Kings 22:1-2**

This is impossible without the Spirit of Wisdom in him. Pick an eight years old child in this contemporary world and crown him King. The implication would be catastrophic without the help of the Holy Spirit. I believe this is obviously the reason our present day empires wait for the child to be grown attaining a level of maturity before being crowned King or Queen. These ones perhaps should have ascended the throne officially years before the actual coronation takes place. Still, it will not be completed without substantial assistance from personal wise counselors and aids. This was the case of

Queen Victoria of the United Kingdom—The Empress of India.

Another practical instance is our LORD JESUS Christ, at age twelve, He sat with learned men of his time, listening and asking questions and they were amazed at his wisdom. I can go on and on with a list without end of other examples. It's important you know that God's wisdom is ageless and timely. He can reveal Himself to you or your child. Pastor Matthew Ashimolowo says it like this, *"It's only a fool who doesn't know that wisdom is ordained in the mouth of a child"*. Without contradiction this statement is very true. In my own experience, whenever our children have presentations to make in the adult church whether drama, choreography or songs and I'm the one taking them, the first thing I do is to layout my plans for them after which I seek their advice. Other times, I ask them to come up with something and when they do, I fly with it. When the accolades start coming in from other teachers, I quickly divert it back to the children or the particular child that gave the idea.

A CHILD'S HUNCH

Respect a child's hunch. Bear the risk to work at it and it may procure more success than a professional's counsel. Many times this one secret has well covered my weaknesses during my years of service as a children's minister. Employ the intelligence of children. Share this testimony with me. Years ago, I was privileged to teach in a home cell fellowship where I was the leader and the wife of the homeowner gave this testimony to the glory of God! She said, the previous day, Saturday she woke up with her legs heavy and she could feel serious pain. Notwithstanding, she tried to stand up but she couldn't. Not knowing exactly what to do, her little son, Jotham (who is also my child in the church) then brought the bottle of anointing oil. He rubbed it on his mom's leg while she was looking at him with surprise. After applying the oil, Jotham prayed a child kind of prayer with in Jesus name amidst it for the mom. The mother was not expecting miracle, but that is when the miracle happened and she was healed.

God is no respecter of a person's size or age.

God our miracle worker is no respecter of persons in size or age. He uses any available vessel including children that will listen to Him. This woman's miracle came firstly because she allowed her child to anoint her and pray for her as any adult would. Countless times children have given me dramas, songs and dance steps that I couldn't have come up with myself. One that is especially stands out of the children I knew then is Karen. Karen is now a successful grown youth applying for her college studies in Nigeria. She is gifted in creative writings as with many other children in the different local assembly I ministered, although I am unable to mention their names.

ESSENCE OF INTERACTIVE CHURCH

Children need to be given the opportunity to express their opinions and ideas. When this participation is encouraged, the teacher will learn from them as well. When children understand your lessons it is important to make room for their contributions in the course of the lesson.

I was privileged to work with two colleagues of mine in a children's class of ten year olds in one of the church a few years back. During the Sunday school class, the children persistently engaged in secret conversations, disrupting the class, even through our best efforts to instill peace in the classroom, we clearly failed. This behavior is almost the norm for kids when they are in class, especially in church services. The moment you involve them in the lesson everyone wants to talk to the teacher and get their attention instead of the child sitting next to them. Generally adults are mature and therefore focused on the teacher and learning while in a classroom situation. But with children their attention span is shorter and they require lively interactions to maintain an order and calmness in the classroom, while they learn.

Children classes must be lively and interactive to be successful.

The children are not the only ones that can become bored in class. Teachers must be aware of their own methods of presentation, if you yourself are sensing bored what do you think the children are feeling? When some of the children are sleeping during the lesson and or others want to use the rest room and all those that are left are only interested in the memory verse. Children are quick at memorizing and that's one reason the memory verse portion of the lesson is a major part of their Sunday school curriculum.

Memorizing Scripture gives the children an understanding of the Bible stories and enable them to quote and apply Bible Scriptures like the adults in daily life situations. As their teacher, you must recognize and humble yourself enough to receive their contributions during the classroom instruction and also after the lesson has been completed. Simply stated children's classes must be **lively** and **interactive** to be successful. To accomplish this task, meekness is required without measure on the part of the teacher. You may find yourself utilizing some of their suggestions and contributions as good instruction tools.

One Sunday in the first church I began my teaching ministry, I was asked to teach the teenagers. This was my first time teaching these teens even though I knew them and had played with them. I didn't teach much and as such, not many of them understood my lesson that day. My poor performance was due to my ignorance about class interaction with this group. I was preaching the same way as I would to adults.

Although you may not be working in children's ministry, it may interest you to know that that day I learned it is far easier to teach adults than children. Do you want to know what really happened in class that day? I was sweating even with two ceiling fans on. A large number of them were in open conversation and I could hardly hear myself think let alone keep any order in the class lesson. When I discovered and applied the secret of class interaction, I was able to carry the students along effortlessly in subsequent services. Walking in meekness with children is like a golden gate of hidden divine knowledge that will assist you in achieving excellent results. Your effectiveness in the testimony out of the mouths of babes will be undeniable to all. (Matthew 11:25, 21:16)

THE PRIDE OF A MINISTER

"Pride goeth before destruction, and an haughty spirit before a fall."
Proverbs 16:18

The pride of a pastor indeed goes before his fall. The opposite of meekness is pride and God hates pride. One of the first principles of a teacher of God, as previously discussed, is that you must always be willing to learn. Develop a mindset that keeps you humble enough to learn from anyone and anything, including toddlers.

Pastor E. A. Adeboye said recently in his daily devotional manual, <u>Open Heaven,</u> said some very penetrating words that will relate perfectly to our discussion here and I quote: *"one thing that can come between you and the divine knowledge that will transform your life is pride."*

That is an amazing statement of warning for those who pride themselves as being full of knowledge while shunning the opinions of others. He further elaborated that God can use vessels you normally would not consider because of their ecclesiastical level, to teach you things that will literally blow your mind. He sealed that statement by saying "this is why you have to remain humble and meek because God can only teach those who are meek." Isn't that what the Scripture speaks about in Psalm 25:9?

It is expedient for you to be humble and have a teachable spirit that you also may learn from the very children you teach. Knowledge does not always coming from the top as you may think. Remember Elihu the son of Barachel the Buzite whose wrath was kindled against Job because he justified himself in his deadly predicament before God. And Job's three friends because they had found no answer and yet had condemned Job. Let's see his reaction in the Holy book. **Job 32:4-9;**

"Now Elihu had waited till Job had spoken, because they were elder than he. When Elihu saw that there was no answer in the mouth of these three men, then his wrath was kindled. And Elihu the son of Barachel the Buzite answered and said, I am young*, and ye are very old; wherefore I was afraid, and durst not shew you mine opinion. I said, Days should speak, and multitude of years should teach wisdom. But there is a spirit in man: and the inspiration of the Almighty giveth them understanding. Great men are not always wise: neither do the aged understand judgment."

Oh my Goodness! Did you see that? The young man made Job understand that as long as you are justifying yourself, you are indirectly saying God is unjust, and God cannot be unjust whether your predicament seems favorably to you or not. God is always true and men are the liars. Until this time that Elihu had come to talk some sense into Job and Job's friends, God kept silent and did not intervene. However when the young man had straightened out all four old men, God broke His silence and affirmed that indeed Elihu had spoken words of wisdom. As you well know, in the aftermath Job received his deliverance and restoration of all things he had previously lost.

God can teach us from any place or person.

I want to stress here emphatically, that maybe what is impeding your next breakthrough in ministry or even in your personal life, is that God has used someone to send you a word in season, but because they appear too inept or familiar to you, you disregard their words by your unbelief. You, therefore, lose the wisdom and breakthrough attached to that instruction. I urge you to remember that where Jesus grew up, the men and women wouldn't receive from Him, because they felt same way you might be feeling. He is just a carpenter's son what does he know? Do not be deceived, we know not as we ought to know and that God's ways are not our ways — He can teach us from anyplace and anything as He sees fit. Wisdom is not an emblem people wear so you can tell who carries the anointing to bless your life and who does not. As you stay meek and humble, the Holy Spirit will help you discern rightly.

As for young men and women, you are to stay humble to an elder speaking only when you are sure it is the Holy Spirit that is nudging you to do so, just like Elihu. God confirms this in is Word in **1 Peter 5:5,**

> **Likewise, ye YOUNGER, submit yourselves unto the ELDER. Yea, all of you (Everybody) be subject one to another, and be clothed with HUMILITY: for GOD resist the PROUD, and giveth grace to the HUMBLE (Meek).**

Chapter Four
Love Them Hate Their Weakness

"And now abideth faith, hope, charity (love); but the greatest of these is charity (love)."
— 1Corinthians 13:13

'Until love is unconditional, there is no Christ in it.'

    The Scripture identifies love as the most potent force in the universe. Love conquers all including unsaved and difficult children. Everyone can be purchased by love no matter how difficult or unruly you may be. Isn't that what the Father used to purchase you and me? Love can cause enemies to become friends and this is why God calls the sun and rain to fall on the just and the unjust—is it because of his generosity or because of His love? God does not do things in the attitude of generosity alone but in the spirit of love. Generosity can be in vain without love. Love always wins.

> **"And though I bestow all my goods to feed the poor, and though I give my body to be burned, and have not charity (love), I am nothing."**
> **1 Corinthians 13:3**

We are to be generous in love even to the most difficult and unsaved children. Take note, when we demonstrate generous love especially to these particular children our rewards will be great.

Most of us demonstrate love better in words than in deeds. We tend to do this primarily because human love has become highly conditional. It is only natural to walk into a class and in less than ten minutes you have a child who has become your favorite. It has happened to me, and it can happen to you. Observation of any teacher will reveal this truth in our nature, even at home between our own children and parents relationships. Usually we are attracted to something with this child, like the child's personality, how they look or respond to you, something you recognize in them you see in yourself, the way a child speaks, or their intelligence and many other things that will cause you to favor this child over another.

Love all children equally.

As small and unimportant as these things may be, to humans they have a vital function that works with our physiology. To deny this truth is to unconsciously and perpetually remain on this side of love that has everything to do with conditions. To be on the divine side of love is not only to accept this truth but to carry Christ in your heart. When Christ is truly in your heart you can love everyone equally. Christ is the image of love. It's imperative that every one in ministry has in them the love of Christ. Recognize your own human weakness to choose one over another. Overcome this tendency by focusing on everyone around the room, irrespective of shortcomings or appearance instead of the individual student that attracts your attention.

WE ARE EMPOWERED TO LOVE

> *"...Because the love of God is shed abroad in our hearts by the Holy Ghost which is given us."*
> Romans 5:5

LOVE
This is one of the ministries of the Holy Spirit that every believer must receive. Don't forget, the Holy Spirit that has been given to us as promised by Christ Jesus, and He will empower you. This empowerment will enable you to implement these standards becoming excellent and effective in your own children's ministry. One very key way to do that is allowing you to see and love peoples regardless of their sins and shortcomings. To actually see people as God sees them. This is difficult to do, and we are unable to accomplish this in our own strength. It is why Jesus said the Holy Spirit will come, the Comforter, and told us with Him we will do greater things. It is not human to love your enemies or people who do not live up to our standards. When we ask the Holy Spirit to help us, He does. This is the testimony of our Christian faith and gives glory to Father God when we love one another as the Lord instructed— this we cannot do on our own.

DIFFICULT CHILDREN

Rampant amongst mankind today, we find it hard to love people without prejudice. It ought not to be so if we have the love of Christ. In most situations, we find it much easier to love those who deserve our love probably for the regard or high esteem they have shown towards us. Narrowing it down to our purpose, love is what every person in ministry must show to every child, irrespective of whether they are your students or not.

To tell you the truth, ministering to difficult children is very difficult. No one volunteers to teach these students. No one can teach these students by their own ability but through the help of the Holy Spirit. Remember, the Holy Spirit shows us how to love and this where you will really need Him. We need to ask the Holy Spirit for wisdom in each case.

Difficult children are kids who will never obey class rules, show interest in what others are learning and are often full of other misdemeanors. It is difficult not to keep track of all the wrong doings especially if you are a disciplinarian like me. We must look past all that in them, because it is the enemy that is hard at work in them, unknowing to the child. **Hate the enemy not the child.** We have been given the keys of the kingdom to cast away the enemy from us. In the case where it's an attitude issue, we should use the weapon of love to help them overcome it. Children are synonymous with throwing tantrums, and we must know when to apply love and when to use the rod—discernment is a key. Many of us are stubborn, arrogant, rude, with many attitude issues and even so, God sacrificially gave his only begotten son for us. That sacrifice is even more amazing when we recognize we are a people who are unworthy to receive such a sacrifice. But God who is all-knowing and all wise knew that the perfect weapon to win over a sinful and unrepentant people is to give them his unfailing love, even when we do not deserve it. People gravitate towards that like a lottery. We need to look at others as God looks at us. We are all unworthy. Who are we to judge the behavior of others? We sit up and take notice when we receive things we know we do not deserve. Children are the same.

Ask the Holy Spirit for wisdom with difficult children.

As a children's minister, when you notice a difficult child in church, find a place and make time to sit with them privately and water them with the Word of God. Giving them attention in this way demonstrates the love you have for this child. This is not the time for a stern rebuke openly before the other children.

LOOK BEYOND THEIR WEAKNESS

"Too guilty to be counted in, but too faithful to be counted out"
—Max Lucado

This statement refers to Peter, one of Jesus's disciples. Christ Jesus didn't focus on the weakness of Peter in denying Him three times. Instead He saw a strong and faithful man who will carry His gospel across Jerusalem into a massive harvest of souls for the Kingdom of God. I love the title Max Lucado called this book *"No Wonder They Called Him Savior."* That is it in a nutshell. God doesn't see as we see, neither does He think as we think. God see's in us who He is called us to be, in His strength not our weakness, His purpose not our mistakes, His talents and gifts and not our failures. He uses the things that sound foolish to the wise in order to confound them and bring glory to Him. Look at the life of the great apostle Paul, not one of us will qualify him to preach the gospel yet his tremendous missionary work carried the gospel of Christ beyond the boundaries of anything that could be equaled today. Moses was a murderer yet God wouldn't use another man for his place. The list of people with histories of failures, mistakes, weaknesses and sins God used mightily is includes almost everyone in the Bible. We would have never hired them to work in our businesses, schools or churches. Yet the one that sees the end from the beginning, that knows what He has predestined us to be, always sees us differently from what men tag us as. It is the enemy that has perverted our way of thinking that raises us above others—that say we are not as bad and deserve more that others.

Effective ministers are people who look beyond a child's weakness or sin to embrace their hidden strength. Look at who they can be with the right teaching or instruction instead of whom they present themselves to be now. God has taught meek men and women His ways just like He did with Moses. The Bible records that Moses was the meekest amongst all the men. Ministers, parents and guardians try to find the gifts and callings in a child's life and see how you can mentor them to find their place in God's kingdom through the strength and power of love.

THIS IS THE FIRST AND GREAT COMMANDMENT

> "Thou shalt love the Lord thy God with all thy heart, and with all thy soul, and with all thy mind. This is the first and great commandment. And the second is like unto it, Thou shalt love thy neighbour as thyself. On these two commandments hang all the law and the prophets."
> Matthew 22:37-40

This is the first and great commandment given to all who believe in the Son. We are to keep the commandments from the Lord, who is the owner of our lives, whether it is convenient to do so or not. I have come across children that ordinarily I would not like let alone love them because of their bad attitudes and forwardness. The love of God and Holy Spirit in me helped me in such times to overcome this error in my judgment. It becomes easier for us to discipline ourselves to start to love all especially when we know this is a requirement for entering the kingdom of heaven—a place we are all waiting to go to. Pray with the Spirit in you, the Holy Spirit always and keep the Lord's commandments—King Solomon said it is our sole duty on earth.

Chapter Five

Be a Cheerful Giver

"Every man according as he purposeth in heart, so let him give; not grudgingly, or of necessity: for God loveth a cheerful giver."
2 Corinthians 9:7

"You can give without loving, but you cannot love without giving"
—David O. Oyedepo

Do you want to know? Children love a cheerful giver, and of course nobody hates a cheerful giver. Isn't that the truth? Truly, you need to love the children in your ministry with open hands, without restraint.

GIFTS

I'm yet to find a child who is not interested in receiving presents. I don't mean ostentatious gifts but from my survey most kids who have taken an interest in me likely began because they experienced how open my hands were to them. You will agree with me that children are always asking, "What did you bring me?" "Buy me some candy." "Can I have your pen?" Children will speak openly like this when they are in the company of their parents or guardians whom they love and feel somewhat of a degree of freedom. This includes teachers. I believe that, the importance that God places on obedience is the magnitude of what receiving a gift means to a child. With that, I strongly mean the value. It may be a little cheap toy, a biscuit, a chocolate or candy but to them it's everything and they greatly appreciate it. Sooner or later you'll discover that the language of love to a child is receiving gifts. Until you give a child a gift, the child cannot really feel you love him or her.

CHILDREN'S PERSPECTIVE OF LOVE

Children have an innate feeling that if adults love them they will provide for their needs whether thy have the resources or not. That is all they know from the beginning as babes. That's funny right? Maybe it is to us as adults but not to them. If you know that a child truly needs something even when they didn't ask, but you have the resources to purchase it for them you should do so. Providing of course it is agreeable to their parents or guardians. Anyway, this is not only applicable to children but everyone including you, because one undeniable demonstration of love is GIVING. The truth in Scripture puts it this way:

> **"...and every man (children inclusive) is a friend to him that giveth gifts."** (Emphasis mine)
> Proverbs 19:6

A REWARD SYSTEM

Ministers, to be effective in teaching children, learn not to hold tight on the blessings God has given you per time. Sometimes what God has provided to you is for the purpose to give to another and not for you at all. But let me also state that as much as your hands are like open doors to kids, giving gifts should be used as a major reward system for children's efforts, either in their academics or spiritual exercise. It is also very important you have enough that will go round your entire class. This should be a tool to be used for rewarding excellence. Remember embracing all is a proof of true Christian love in your heart. So let them know the system ahead of time that they may work towards the goals you set. The guidelines to receive a reward will be when they do well in their academics, start demonstrating godliness in areas of respect, responsibility, or showing more interest in kingdom advancement as examples. You can increase your list are you are led by the Holy Spirit to do.

BIRTHDAYS ARE ALSO CHANNELS FOR GIFTS

Remembering a child's birthdays with a paper birthday card is also a colorful gift in disguise. The card may also be signed by other children as a great surprise and to the delight of the recipient.

Practically, be sensitive to each child's heart's desire and give gifts accordingly. I'm saying this because sometime ago I bought a nice leather wristwatch for a child on her birthday. She appeared to greatly appreciate it even her parents came to thank me for this kindness. But… she never wore it to church to show it off as I expected she would. I had thought she needed a watch since I have not seen her with one. She had let me know when it was her birthday. I later found out that she really didn't want a wristwatch for her birthday but that she was expecting something else. Although she was polite and thankful, I wasn't aware in her heart she said, "Oh no, a watch, I so wanted a doll." Their choice is not your choice so buy them what you know they will like. If you have no foreknowledge of their desires and interests, find out from other reliable sources, keep track in a note pad, especially if you wish to make it a surprise for them.

Remember their birthdays with gifts.

Most importantly, it is not only considerate of you if you remember their birthdays without their reminder, but these kindnesses are also an astute thing to do as their teacher. I guess you may know their parents will be made aware of your gesture, and God will record it against your goodwill too. This is a great step to begin to foster better Christian relationships between you and the children and their families. To make this possible you may need a class birthday reminder or some other e-calendar methods you can create in your laptop or diary. Reminding them of your own birthday using paper cards will lighten your spirit and bring much joy that you will not soon forget throughout your lifetime. The ones I have received on my birthdays are more than just funny papers. Instead I receive them as prophecy. I treasure those paper cut out cards and the words chosen by these little ones for me. One year my fellow Christian teachers saw a birthday card given to me by one of the children. They laughed and laughed. Occasionally, I bring them out to read, and I am filled again with joy as I chuckle at them nonstop. Always remember their birthdays but don't expect them to always remember yours. So don't be surprised when they do not remember. Let them know ahead of time if you care for their surprises like me.

ALWAYS KEEP YOUR PROMISES

Promising of gifts is allowed even if you must delay because of financial constraint. Never deny them the gift you promised albeit late. They may forget you promised them a gift, but don't you forget that you made the promise. It is important to keep your word, your integrity before the child. Someday you may have to make a bigger promise to that same child, or teach that child the definition of a promise from the Bible. Always look for opportunities to strengthen the examples and lessons, applying the Word in everyday life. These little things matter greatly to children and even most adults. Finally, know that there is no limit to the extent you should give gifts, if it means giving gifts everyday and if you can afford it then do it. Children love gifts. We should all be the kind of minister that love giving good gifts to our children as our Heavenly Father gives good gifts to us. It should not be a difficult thing for you to show concern over their welfare and their family when you have been blessed in that capacity.

> "I have compassion on the multitude, because they have now been with me three days, and have nothing to eat."
> Matthew 8:2

Jesus had compassion on them and did not send them away hungry, what prevents you from feeding the children with chocolate and other treats that you can afford. Job said:

> "I was an eye to the blind, and feet was I to the lame. I was a father to the poor: and the cause which I knew not I searched out."
> Job 29:15-16

BENEFITS OF GIVING

> "There is that scattereth, and yet increaseth; and this that withholdeth more than is meet but it tendeth to poverty."
> Proverbs 11:24

The benefits of giving are so numerous. They return to us in multiple ways of health, long life, protection, favor, actual finances and many more I may not be able to list here. All in all, it creates room for trans-generational blessings. The Scripture in **Hebrews 6:10** reveals;

"For God is not unrighteous to forget your work and labour of love, which ye have shown toward his name, in that ye have ministered to the saints (children), and do minister."

Much of the things I enjoy in my ministry today are rewards from God from things that I have done previously in children's ministry, for God's kingdom generally and still that I am doing. In my little ways, I fed children, clothed them, took them to hospital, paid their fees and still support the children's church in other ways financially. I never tire of doing so. It has become part of my everyday life, which I thoroughly enjoy. Your giving or lack of giving, will always multiply back to you, just like a boomerang! What you sow you will invariably reap.

Love is a boomerang!

Chapter Six

Build family friendship

"Thine own friend, and thy father's friend, forsake not; neither go into thy brother's house in the day of thy calamity: for better is a neighbor that is near than a brother far off."
Proverbs 27:10

"What do you do with a friend? You stick by him"
—Max Lucado

FAMILY FRIENDSHIP

Building family friendships is important to you in ministry and to parents. There is an increased demand as well as a sacrifice of your time working with the whole family. Even if you come across proud and unfriendly parents this should not deter your effort to be effective as a pastor. Whatever may be the case it will require you to manage the plight, whether tight schedules or unfriendly parents. The old cliché says, "Charity begins at home." In children's ministry you may need to have established ties with the parents especially those posing concern to you either in their Christian character or academics.

Love begins in the home.

VISIT THEIR HOMES OCCASIONALLY

Sometimes before you can impart into a child's life, you may need to know him closely either from the home or church. This is why many parents try to personally put their child under the teachers care when the child is within the walls of the school. As a teacher, you are required to get to know the child's short comings if you truly care what becomes of them in the future. I must warn you, you will never know the total child by your relationship with that child outside their home. I can tell because I was once a child in children church and later became a teacher.

As a child, we will hide our spots from our teachers behavioral truths will only be revealed by our parents. We were in fear that we would be found out and that our teacher would learn of our shortcomings whether at school or church. It takes a family friendship to know them well and what spots they have hidden if any.

One Saturday while visiting children at their home, I was able to meet with the mother along with the children. The parents do not attend our church and these children usually come late for services. We spent some time singing praises together and praying. Then I asked their mom if they do morning devotional prayers in the house, and she said not regularly. She also said most times when they wake up to pray, these children sleep late, and she needs to wake them up, especially the eldest boy. In our culture the eldest should be more serious and be a pathfinder for the other younger siblings. After everything, I specifically counseled this boy and by the grace of God I know he's a changed young man today.

Remember, you will never know the **total child** until you see them in their home.

CREATE OPPORTUNITY FOR FRIENDSHIP

An effective minister continues to seek additional ways to effect a positive change in a child's life. Don't give up on this point as you well know true friendship will always take time to build. George Washington said, *"True friendship is a plant of slow growth, it must undergo and withstand the shocks of adversity, before it is entitled for is appellation."*

If you really want to mold and instill Christian character in a child you must find opportunity to form family ties with this child. If they or their parents don't come to you as friend you must take the initiative to develop friendship towards them. By so doing you might be creating a covenant friendship just like Jonathan did for David.

Take initiative to befriend their family.

I like the way Milton Berle puts it: *"if opportunity doesn't knock, build a door."* Your friendship with a family will undergo trials but stay in it and don't quit too soon. In my own experience, most parents have made it easier for me by coming to meet me. They have concerns about their child's plight academically or his poor Christian character. The child has demonstrated this at home or some kids have complained about their bad attitude without me ever asking them anything. I believe they have confidence in me perhaps as a result of the friendship I have built with them and their home. There were still times when I was the one to take the first step of friendship. I was not rebuffed when I did, rather they became a sweet friendship every step of the way.

FRIENDSHIP BIRTHS TRUST AND TRUST LEADS TO FRIENDSHIP

'Friendship births trust and trust leads to friendship'. This statement is very correct both ways. It is only a matter of time, a friendship you started and was skeptical about it may lead to a true friendship just as the trust you have for someone leads you to want to make them your friends. Children will trust you when they know you are well spoken of in their home. Oftentimes the children in the churches where I ministered will bypass other ministers to talk to me or request me to pray with them. I want you to know that things don't happen inadvertently. I have well done my homework that the children have listed me on their honor rolls. Apart from giving gifts and other things I have deliberately and compassionately listened to them, showed interest in their academics just as I do in their spiritual life and that of their family. Individually I have visited them and regularly telephoned them to check on them and their families.

Love is expressed in true friendship.

SHOW YOURSELF FRIENDLY

Don't be cynical be friendly. Cynical people believe people approach you for friendship out of a negative motive. As a child of God it is best to use discernment by the Spirit of God and exercise compassion especially in new relationships. Do not assume because of previous bad experiences that everyone is like that.

"A man that hath friends must shew himself friendly: and there is a friend that sticketh closer than a brother."
Proverbs 18:24

This is very important. Why would someone want to come and be your friend when your *actions* demonstrate you don't really even *like* people? Generally, people judge by appearances. Only God knows the heart. So for me I regularly engage in warm chats with the parents after church meetings. It brings me closer not only to the family but also to the child in question, which is my ultimate goal. This can be hard I know, but if saving a child is on the top of your priority list, you will enjoy every part of these principles. Other times I have visited homes (in the company of other children mostly) if anyone of them is sick. The reward from the time spent is usually incredible. Effective ministers will not wait for parents to come seeking their help. Instead teachers should follow up with the parents to learn more about the child they are teaching.

In as much as you cannot create a strong and long lasting friendship with every family, then it's required of you at the very least to be friendly with all family. The motive is not about creating strong and lasting friendship with the family (although this can be an added benefit), but primarily finding ways to affect a child's life in a positive way.

"Ye are my friends…"
John 15:14

The Lord Jesus Christ didn't just speak these words he also proved them many times over. One occasion was when Apostle Peter's mother-in-law was sick with a fever, Jesus visited the home of his friend Peter and Jesus healed her. She then got up and began to serve them. Sometimes we need to allow the friendships with the children to go beyond the church or school premises.

Chapter Seven

Practice Patience Beyond Limit

"For ye have need of patience, that, after ye have done the will of God, ye might receive the promise."
Hebrews 10:36

"I was smart enough to understand that to develop patience I would have to go through trials that I didn't want to endure"
—Joyce Meyer

Let me highlight clearly, that the *will* of God here is *teaching the children,* and the *promise* is the *impact* you will later see in their lives. However, let's see how to practice patience beyond limit with children.

PATIENCE

It is wisely declared that patience is a virtue. This means, patience is not common to everyone. We need to strive for it. It is not common yet it's essential for success. Show me a successful man, and I will show you a man who is patient within his pursuits. Likewise for people to be successful in effecting a change in any child's life patience must be deployed. To manage children successfully, patience is required without measure. Most of the time children's attitudes are offensive and annoying. Naturally, many children are quite obstinate and they will need to be reprimanded but this should be done with patience—change comes gradually. What you expect them to understand in a day may take a week, a month even a year. Be calm and take things slowly with them. Never expect positive changes immediately amongst children not even in adults—with adults change maybe gradual sometimes while with children it may really be delayed.

Positive change comes gradually.

Funny enough, though their change is delayed, they are getting it. It may appear they are not following up but you need to practice the act of a slow reaction. Play is in their nature during the young ages. The seventh edition of the *Oxford Advanced Learner's Dictionary* defines patience, "as the ability to stay calm and accept delay or something annoying without complaining". To be candid with yourself, let me ask you, do you think that the practice of patience is easy? I know your answer is 'NO.' I believe that is why the ancients called it a virtue, meaning it's not common and it is hard to acquire. You pay a price to acquire it and if you must succeed with kids you must develop patience without limit.

"And let us not be weary in well doing: for in due season we shall reap, if we faint not."
Galatians 6:9

Without patience you will not like the outcome of your own reaction let alone theirs.

MY EXPERIENCE

Some time ago a teacher I was working with refused to allow a young teenager to participate in our class activity. This was simply because the young teen was quiet in nature and appeared unintelligent to her. I insisted the teen should be allowed to participate. I knew the teen because I have visited her family previously. In conversation with her mom we talked about her school performance. This young girl achieved remarkable reports from school, usually being first in her class. I believed in her ability even though she was acted as an introvert in public. I argued that this student be given a chance. Two or three Sundays later the same teacher who told me she didn't want to include her, walked up to me and whispered in my ear, "Do you know Isioma is catching up." "Yes, she just needed time", I replied. Children can do anything you want them to do as long as you are mild mannered and demonstrate patience toward them.

SELF CONTROL

Many a time, children have surprised me by how they master their lines in drama or even during our Christian debates on Children's Days. The result is usually incredible! Parents, guardians and ministers in children's ministry have experienced this truth over and over again. Children can be very annoying and they know how to push all of your buttons if you are a temperamental person, but you must grasp self-control to win over whatever negative reaction that may result. Scripture tells us in **Proverbs 25:28;**

> **"He that hath no rule over his own spirit is like a city that is broken down, and without walls."**

Virtues can be taken from such city. Diligently guard yourself from what will lead you into wrong reactions because of what a rebellious child will do. There are other options that will prove successful. You can lose your self and damage your reputation when you are caught up in unholy anger. Generally, children will cry for no reason, they jump when they should be calm and yell when they should not be excited. They can be like the weather sometimes you just cannot predict their actions or reactions.

Discernment and understanding of a child's actions is required as the teacher to appropriate the exact measure of discipline, if any. This is what defines your effectiveness. There have been times I have chuckled at their actions when I should have raised my voice to maintain order. Since that time when I noticed my laughter corrects their behavior (even when they have messed up) this has become another one of my valuable tools in training up children.

Never correct a child from a distance.

Never try to correct a child from a distance. This will not work. It is like waiting to receive a signal at the other end of a telephone line when there are no connecting cables or wireless devices. When they are around you then you can give any measure of instruction employed by you as a parent or the authority given you as a minister from the children's church leadership.

Don't get me wrong, I'm a disciplinarian myself as I have previously mentioned but it must be done in love by applying wisdom. Can I tell you something? Every child has a hidden treasure inside of them that their parents cannot afford, not even the wealthiest Mom and Dad. But it takes time for these treasures to be revealed and begin to find expression. No wonder the Scripture says *"He makes everything beautiful at their time."* (Ecclesiastes 3:11).

Be patient in disciplining them especially while correcting their mistakes. Not enough can be said regarding this principle because young people including children lack experience and therefore have lots of shortcomings.

Before becoming a children's teacher I failed miserably with children especially in my relationships with my younger siblings. God started dealing with me and I'm glad to be under His influence and wisdom, which continues to carry through even today. Every great achievement requires unlimited patience especially for those who want to be effective in children's ministry. To get the best from any child, ministers should be slow to action but quick to endure attitudes that can be unbearable from children at any time.

"He that is slow to anger (action) is better than the mighty; and he that ruleth his spirit than he that taketh a city."
Proverb 16:32

Chapter Eight

Be Their Intercessor

"The effectual fervent prayer of a righteous man availeth much."
—James. 5:16b.

Intercede for them;
Stand in the gap for them in prayers.

PRAYER

As religious as the term may sound, I have not seen any person who doesn't believe in prayer, at least not yet. Likely, most everyone will say one form of prayer or another to whom ever or whatever they have their hope in.

Some years ago, I was working in the field to get the subsurface geological report of that area. This was with a small group of students and the lecturer, during my undergraduate final research work. Myself, and one of my classmate stood about 600 meters away from the other students in the bush, sending currents to underground layers to get the geological report. While we were both standing there, a weird looking man came out the inside of the bush and walked up to us. Immediately I was afraid but the Spirit of God in me instantly rose up filling me with confidence and peace.

The man approached us and accused us of standing on the god's of their farmland. This was some kind of giant tree. The moment he informed us he left quickly. Without a word, my classmate and I hurriedly finished our work and left to join the others in the open field. I'm saying this because just as that weird farmer believed in some kind of harvest deity on his farm that he prays to, many people believe in something that they pray to. What I want you to understand here is that, many people pray but *who* they pray to, is what differentiates them.

But as Christians we pray to Father God through our Lord Jesus Christ. We all know that prayer changes things and we should still know that prayer will change our children and mature them into children with strong Christian character.

PRAYER IS THE MASTER'S KEY

> "And the Lord said, Simon, Simon, Satan hath desired to have you, that he may sift you as wheat: But I have prayed for thee, that thy faith fail not: and when thou art converted, strengthen thy brethren."
> Luke 22:31-32

Do you see that? The enemy's desire is to sift those ones who have a mission in The Lord's Kingdom by perverting their attitude. As ministers we must stand up in prayer for them just as in this example the Lord has done for Peter, asking him to strengthen his brethren. You too have a responsibility to strengthen these children during your own personal prayer time and during corporate prayer. As we have seen from the above Scripture, prayer is Jesus's key to winning the battle for his disciples over the enemy—follow the examples of our Lord.

IMPORTUNITY PRAYER

> *"Winners don't quit and quitters don't win"*
> —Oral Roberts

Some of the vices and habits the children have been perverted with will not leave them by a onetime prayer. You will have to tarry long in the place of prayer for them never giving up but always persisting. This is very important for the children's church leadership. During your corporate prayer meetings let these issues become some of your prayer lines, mention the names of the children whom you would love to see changes in their character. Take it to God in prayer and keep at it, for God always answers persistent people.

> **"And he said unto them, which of you shall have a friend, and shall go unto him at midnight, and say unto him, friend, lend me three loaves; For a friend of mine in his journey is come to me, and I have nothing to set before him? And he from within shall answer and say, trouble me not: the door is now shut, and my children are with me in bed; I cannot rise and give thee I say unto you, though he will not rise**

and give him, because he is his friend, yet because of his importunity he will rise and give him as many as he needeth."
Luke 11:5-8

Why did you think the Lord gave this parable? This is not given just for our enjoyment in the reading. Of course not! It is given to us because there will be issues in our life that will require more than a one time prayer. We are called to pray without ceasing believing to receive what has been given to you in Christ Jesus. This is the way as children's ministers we ought to pray for difficult and unruly children in our churches. Keep praying and you will surely see the answer—though it may tarry but wait for the change for it will not tarry more than necessary.

PRAY FOR THEM THAT ARE SICK

"Is any sick among you? Let him call for the elders of the church; and let them pray over him, anointing him with oil in the name of the Lord: And the prayer of faith shall save the sick, and the Lord shall raise him up; and if he have committed sins, they shall be forgiven him."
James 5:14-15

I can't count the number of times children have walked up to me saying, "Uncle, I'm not feeling well." Then I ask them, "What is the problem, do you have pain?" I quickly say a short, simple prayer for healing. Before you know it Jesus has healed them, without needing any referrals to the medical unit. Soon you will see the same child actively playing in the church assembly or participating in various activities. At other times, when I notice their passiveness and quiet demeanor I approach them and they confide in me what the problem is. What else can I do except pray for them and allow Jesus to do the healing.

Likewise, in the issue of their academics, when I finish counseling them then I pray and ask God to take total control with testimonies following later. To God I give all the glory forever! There is no limit to the potency of prayer. It is important not to forget to pray for the children on a regular basis. To be successful in children's ministry you must pray for them and allow God's glory to be manifest through them.

PRAYER ROOM

> "And when thou prayest, thou shalt not be as the hypocrites are: for they love to pray standing in the synagogues and in the corners of the streets, that they may be seen of men. Verily I say unto you, they have their reward. BUT THOU, when THOU prayest, enter into thy CLOSET, and when thou hast shut thy door, pray to thy Father which is in secret; and thy Father which seeth in secret shall reward thee openly."
> **Matthew 6:5-6**

More importantly is your prayers done in secret for these children that matters the most to God. While you pray for them seek their salvation first in to God's kingdom and then their social wellbeing. Any child that is first saved can overcome any limitations, although it may take time victory is certain. Time spent in your prayer room will reveal new insights and ideas that you can utilize in your classes and throughout your everyday activities. We know that nothing frustrates children like too much routine, however nothing excites them more than a change in activities. In other words to pass their test you must be creative and innovative.

Prayer carries spiritual power to transform any child. Until you have prayed and fasted regularly for the life of the children you teach you will not see a change in that child's life. Consequently, you must be a righteous intercessor in much for prayer to bring positive results. Pursue holiness with your heart and God's presence around you will protect the children around you.

Prayer carries spiritual power to transform any child.

Chapter Nine

Embrace All Children

"What man of you, having an hundred sheep, if he lose one of them, doth not leave the ninety and nine in the wilderness, and go after that which is lost, until he find it."
Luke 15:4

**"When you ignore people,
you only ignore what they will become."
—Myles Munroe**

EMBRACE ALL

Include all of the children when you are demonstrating your love and while recognizing the reciprocation of that love. Always remember the action of a mother hen, as she guards *all* her chicks against beasts and when it rains she sets her feather to cover them *all*. Many people in children's ministry abandon the children because of poor performance or unruly attitudes of these children. It is the responsibility of those in children's ministry to make improvements in these children's lives. This is a warning. This should not happen with your kids. History is full of men and women who were abandoned by their teacher and as a result of their weaknesses in the early days of their education. Regrettably, some of them never made it in life and were unsuccessful as adults as a direct result of their teacher's wrong attitude towards them. Not all of these children fail though, history is also full of men and women who were rejected by their teachers and others but overcame these obstacles in their lives. As a teacher we need to avoid abusive words and actions towards the children.

FATHER OF ALL

As a minister it is easy to show kindness and attention to those kids who obey you, or are the astute or possibly from wealthy families. Do not get led down this path. Love all, cover all and embrace all. True Christian love is not partial. Demonstrate your love and attention to them all. The Scripture tells us our Heavenly Father is a Father to all.

> **"One God and Father of all, who is above all, and through all, and in you all."**
> **Ephesians 4:6**

Therefore, you must be a minister to all if you want to be effective.

Quite by mistake I had an incident of this very principle sometime ago while teaching in our children church. A boy of about nine years old once confronted me and said, "Uncle, you don't love me." He felt that I didn't pay any attention to him. I would ask the class to raise their hands of who had an answer to my questions. Generally more hands went up than what I needed to elaborate my lesson. I would choose from two or three students. According to the boy, I didn't choose him. Worse, this wasn't the first or second time I had not chosen him and thereby ignored him. He said it so sincerely that I really felt I had been partial to him. I made a point to try to make him feel loved during the rest part of the Sunday school class. To further convince him that I loved him, after the service I pressed upon him to understand that I loved him and every other child equally. This goes beyond words since the proof of love is in deeds not just in words.

Love all, cover all, and embrace all!

I love bold kids like him. He is now a teenager and living in the same town where my parents reside. On occasion, I still get to visit with him. I continue to speak affirmations into his life in the ways of the Lord, building on what was previously taught at children's church.

Some of us as adults may see folly in children. Still children are very sensitive to your actions and watch you very closely. I believe it's wisely said that, 'parents are mirrors to their children.' They watch you and mimic your ways.

Whatever you do for one, do also for all. You are not assigned to the class just to be somebody's coach but rather to be everybody's teacher. To those of you who are paid teachers at regular schools to teach, know that you are not paid to render your services to only your favorite kids or those that obey you. Therefore, neglect no child nor leave any behind. If children don't understand, it is your duty as a teacher to teach them to give them understanding of their lessons. You are being paid to teach the entire class. Be patient with all of them and soon you will begin to see the fruit of your labor in the success of your student's achievements. This also reflects well on your experience and abilities for future assignments as a teacher.

GOD IS WATCHING US

Not only the children know you have failed to embrace them, but your Father in Heaven knows and you won't be a part of that child's success story. I cannot stipulate this enough, whatsoever you give to one child give to the other children too. Discipline yourself with this warning from our Lord Jesus Christ

> **"But whoso shall offend one of these little ones which believe in me, it were better for him that a millstone were hanged about his neck, and that he were drowned in the depth of the sea".**
> **Matthew 18:6**

The day I received understanding of this Scripture as it applies to me, I personally asked God for grace that I would never offend any child. If I am too hurried, I am quick to apologize with these words, "I'm sorry dear." The consequences are unbearable. No one is immune from receiving the judgment from the hand of Christ. When you show special attention to some children, it does not only offend that child, it can also offend other children in the classroom and ultimately Christ is highly offended at your behavior. In other words, as you embrace them all, you embrace Christ likeness in disguise.

Neglect no child nor leave any behind.

Chapter Ten

Catch a Personal Vision for Them

"But a child left to himself bringeth his mother shame... Where there is no vision, the people perish: but he that keepeth the law, happy is he."
Proverbs 29:15, 18

Vision is the unveiling of God's plan for us. The plans and purposes of God for His children are always to give them a great and colorful end. And every child of God must come to the understanding and belief that God's intent for them regardless of their plight at anytime is to bring them to success. The children of Israel were in captivity, yet God still spoke through Prophet Jeremiah that they should build houses, get married, marry off their daughters, and takes wives for their sons. He had a great plan to multiply them even in their captivity so that by the time they are returning from captivity they will return in their multiplied state numerically, materially and otherwise. From the Scripture, you will affirm that God always has great plans for anything He has called us to do for Him. If God has called you into children's ministry either for a season or as a lifelong occupation—there is a perfect plan in His mind for that. There is something He has called you to do personally for His kids aside from the church corporate vision. As long as you place God's will, first and foremost, there will be no confusion.

Following the Lord and listening to His direction regarding your own personal will fit together as one and the same for whatever church He has led you to. All in all, so long as your vision is indeed from God, He will lead you to as part of His body to go into the world and teach. We must always follow the Lord's commands and not the diluted and twisted doctrines of devils available almost everywhere today.

What I mean is that, we are all part of the body of Christ. We have been given different gifts, callings, using various methods and strategies to achieve His will. Every ministry should evangelize, making disciples and transforming lives through the Gospel of Jesus Christ. Because we are uniquely designed by our Creator, we end up accomplishing the same goals but differently with our various gifts as God has ordained it. In any case, you can be sure that Jesus Christ is the model of what we need to be doing. He is the authors and finisher of what we believe and teach.

DISCOVER HIS PLAN FOR YOU

> *"It is the glory of God to conceal a thing: but the honour of kings is to search out a matter."*
> **Proverbs 25:2**

Christ Jesus has already redeemed you and me to be Kings and priest to reign on the earth. (Revelation 5:10). Scripture reveals who we are in Christ. I believe this is true and you should too. God cannot lie. If He says this is what He sees, then believe it that that *is* what He sees, regardless of how you see yourself. Your position will not change what the Scripture reveals nor will God change his mind. So as a king, search out what God has already concealed, even before you were born, concerning you.

God has already predetermined a perfect plan for you. Your responsibility is to discover it. Find out from Him what it is. Does he want you to raise children for him? Who will be the next Timothy, or David Oyedepo, or Billy Graham? Perhaps He has empowered you to lead his children to his Kingdom while they are young; preparing them as an adoring bride for the coming of the groom. Whatever His plans are for planting you in the children's ministry or bringing that child into your path, as a parent or a spiritual parent, it is your obligation to find out and begin running with it.

WAYS TO DISCOVER YOUR VISION

There are several ways to find out from God what He has for us. Though, some of us will encounter God's will for our lives by God's *happenstance* like Moses or Paul, this is not always the case for every child of God.

You need to study and search the **Word**. The Word will reveal not just who you are but who God is. Once you understand who God is and the desires of His heart you will come to better understand His will and calling for you. There are no shortcuts to studying the Word. The Word is a mirror, as we look at it we are able to see who we really are.

Prayer is a platform we need to utilize daily for asking and receiving input from God regarding our divine path and plans for our lives.

"Call unto me, and I will answer thee, and shew thee great and mighty things, which thou knowest not."
Jeremiah 33:3

Ask in prayer and expect the answers… in His time and not yours. Others will come along side of you using their *passions* and *gifts* to help you grow and mature. You will come to know God places *people* in your path every step of the way to help and encourage you. You are not alone in God's kingdom.

There are no shortcuts to studying the Word.

The more you learn about God the more you will hunger and thirst for Him. Your appetite will increase as in any relationship. Until you feel desperate for more of Him you have not gotten serious about your future. God knows when you desperate.

Some years back, a bosom friend of mine said to me, "It's good for you that you know God's plan for your life but for me I do not." "Ask Him, I replied." "I have been asking Him for several years now," he said. Although a person may have a desire for more of God, they are not yet *desperate* for Him. These are two different things.

Scripture cannot be broken and does not lie. (Jeremiah 33:3).

If God said He says it, then of course He will do it. When you are desperate, there is a point where there are no other options for you living a satisfied life except by God. This is the point where God knows you are serious about your search for Him, and He will reveal Himself to you. You will know that you know, it *is* God and no other. Ask with persistence. Continue asking until you have received. See an example of this persistence carried out in Luke 11:5–13.

CORPORATE VISION

Every ministry has a vision, whether adults, teens, children's ministry or any other church ministry group which is being used for the advancing of God's Kingdom here on earth.

The Lord has led me to establish my current ministry, *Millennium Christian Ministry*, and our vision is as follows:

Millennium Christian Ministry is commissioned to remove the shame and reproach of the people in the African community through the preaching of the Gospel of Jesus Christ; and in doing so: We will save souls and help believers grow into the fullness of Christ, help the impoverished, and raise Nehemiahs' for Christ that will champion the reform that Africa needs.

It's so important that every ministry and people should find and run with their divine vision instead of their own desires. Every divine vision will attract divine support from God's in His perfect timing. God will also provide you with all the strength and ability to endure and surmount obstacles that surely appear along your way. If you are following your own vain vision or path, do not expect God to help you through it, neither support you—this is why hearing it from God cannot be underestimated.

You can personalize the corporate vision of your church where you teach children and run with it as your own. This will even make you very effective as you serve God and His children in that ministry. When you join a ministry, it is expected you walk in their vision. If you are in disagreement with your church's vision or calling why are you attending that church in the first place? Soon you become rebellious and the sin of rebellion is equal to witchcraft. No one wants that.

When you join a ministry, it is expected you walk in their vision.

God has a church for you where the vision He has given you will fit like a glove to the vision He has given the church he has placed you in. It is up to you to find that church and discover God's plan for you and for the children from that ministry. The Holy Spirit will begin confirming your vision through you and through the children. You must understand that it's only when you personalize the vision that it will stir your heart and grow. A man of vision is a passionate and tireless man.

He moves against all odds and still gets accomplishes all he has set out to do successfully.

> **"I will stand upon my watch, and set me upon the tower, and will watch to see what he will say unto me, and what I shall answer when I am reproved. And the LORD answered me, and said, write the vision, and make it plain upon tables, that he may run that readeth it. For the vision is yet for an appointed time, but at the end it shall speak, and not lie: though it tarry, wait for it; it will surely come. It will not tarry."**
> **Habakkuk 2:1-3**

Read this Scripture again and underline the phrase *that he may run that read it.* Did you notice that? The scripture never said that *'they'* may run that read it but instead it says *'he'* may run that reads. This is a revealed knowledge.

Bring your children's ministers to the point of *'he'* in the corporate vision whether they came in with their own vision or not – the corporate vision should serve as a sponge for all.

VISION BIRTHS EXCELLENCE

>"When you see the invisible,
>you will do the impossible"
>—Oral Roberts

I fully and heartily agree with these words of the great evangelist. I began this chapter by saying vision is the beginning of every great achievement either in God's kingdom or in the secular world as it were. Our being effective as children's minister begins by first catching a personal vision for these children. This is a watermark for sure between those who end up being effective and those who do not. When you see it, you strive passionately to become it. The people who were building the tower of Babel saw what they wanted to build and nothing could restrain them from building that edifice until God and the host of heaven came down to stop the project. Glory to God that He will not stop what is done in the name of Jesus Christ, which will bring Him glory. To raise children of excellence you must first visualize it in your mind's eye and work at it diligently. The vision will surely speak at the end. Don't get discouraged when you don't see any impact at beginning. The scripture never said it would speak at the beginning. It said at the *end* it shall speak and not tarry.

> "Vision is a source of hope;
> it is the source of courage; it's the source of
> perseverance in the midst of difficulty."
> —Myles Munroe

VISION GUIDES

Vision statements will act as a guide to keep you focused and on track. Distractions will come. Distractions find all men, and you can only overcome them by sticking closely to your guide. Some distractions will come in the form of offences received from other ministers you are serving alongside. The enemy will use this to weary you and undermine the good plans God has for the children through you. A man with a vision will look away from all of that and follow his guide.

As a geologist back in my college days, we would go on field mapping trips. We would be given a base map indicating all the geological features to be mapped, and the routes to be used to and from that location. God help you if you ever lost that base map! Although you could eventually get back to your base camp with the help of a GPS or compass, but you would not achieve the results expected when you set out. You would no longer be able to identify the locations where those features are on your map. This is just like what vision accomplishes for us.

Catch a personal vision for the children.

Vision guides you, just like the base map of the earth that scientists use. It enables you to know where your divine features are and how to reach them—the end goals. So in the field, as we move with this base map, we do not stop randomly looking at various earth features, it would be a waste of time and prevent us from finishing the given assignment as indicated on the map. Randomly stopping is similar to the actions of a tourist while sightseeing. They usually have no specific goals outside of satisfying their desires with beautiful sights. A man of vision avoids time wasting distractions and instead placing the goal first. The moment you set out to do something effectively for God, the enemy will attack you through many forms to try and stop you. I encourage you not to give in to him, keep your eyes on the prize, and soon he will leave you just as he left the Lord Jesus Christ.

MY VISION

> *"...They shall mount up with wings as eagles..."*
> Isaiah 40:31

Personally, this is my vision for every child I have ever taught while in children's ministry. This is still true today as I pastor both the children God brings to me at *Millennium Christian Church*. As we continue to grow in all aspects of a church and others come along side with us, it will continue to serve as the corporate vision for our children. We wish to raise children who will *fly like the eagle* among their peers both spiritually and intellectually; children who will climb the mountains in their spiritual walk with our Lord Jesus Christ and who will wear crowns of excellence in their academics and later in their life endeavors.

I have always desired to raise children of excellence both at the church and the home front. What eagles are to other birds is what I want the children I am privileged to teach to become. Better than their peers. The eagle is the King of the Air, as Lion is the King of the Jungle. In my seven active years of teaching children, I can't say I have got to the mountain top with every kid I taught, but glory to God some are now teenagers who are already flying. Now I have been given a much larger responsibility for the children God will bring to *Millennium Christian Ministries*. Although I now serve as the church pastor, children's ministry will always be an integral part of my life. As much as is possible I will continue to teach children and give my full assistance to all children's ministers in our church. I will continue to ask for the Lord's grace to do so.

Keep your eyes on the prize!

EPILOGUE

Being effective is not so much of a question of whom you teach or what you teach, but it is a question of how you teach the things and people you teach. Therefore, if you cannot effect a change in their lives, find out why you are not being effective.

In other words, you haven't learned these salient principles enough to become *effective* as a children's teacher. Perhaps, you have not applied the acquired knowledge well enough. Even in my short experience, I've learned that until knowledge is practically applied it is of no value. Napoleon Hill said in his book, *Think and Grow Rich*, "Men are paid, not merely for what they know, but more particular for what they do with that which they know." Without any sense of debating this truth, you will agree with me that what you know doesn't make you *effective* as a children's teacher rather what makes you *effective* is what you do with that which you know—this is know as applied knowledge.

To apply this knowledge you must master regular patterns for your teaching. To every potential children's teacher, I want to say don't be afraid, teaching children can be great fun for you. You don't want to miss the joy you will experience. Times without number, I've openly told other members at *Living Faith Church* while in ministry there, that there is no any other arm of the Church I am interested in except the children's ministry. Of course that is allowing for the desires of the Almighty God who may want me elsewhere.

To those of you out there who may think you would never want to teach children, for whatever reason, let me tell you this; you are missing out a on a great and fulfilling ministry. Remember also you will be required one day to teach your own kids. This task is unavoidable. If we embrace this task with joy today we will together not only save these little ones for Jesus, but we will be growing up the next generation of good Christians increasing the Kingdom of God worldwide if Jesus tarries.

Let me end with the words of this man, Fyodor Dostoyevsky, *"The soul is healed by being with children."* Effective teachers are people who enjoy being with children. If you are a person who doesn't enjoy being with children, these principles will not work for you no matter how much effort you make.

Enjoying what you do, walking in the plan God has planned for you and listening to the prompting of the Holy Spirit is what works with these salient principles to deliver the ultimate—EFFECTIVE CHILDREN'S MINISTRY.

Until knowledge is practically applied, it is of no value.

My First Day as a Children's Teacher

So you are considering becoming a teacher! Maybe you have thought about teaching in the children assembly but are not sure where to begin. Here are some lessons from some of my first days as a teacher in Sunday school.

It was a beautiful Sunday morning, and there were hundreds of children and teachers present in the assembly. On one hand, I was confidently enthusiastic, but on the other hand, my heart was beating with fear. I was enthusiastic because of my passion for teaching but also had fear and lots of thoughts running through my mind. Perhaps I was afraid for my lack of teaching experience in the church, even though I was currently employed as a teacher at that time in a government secondary school under national assignment. This was a compulsory assignment for every graduate by the Nigeria government as a way of national integration of her citizens.

I realized that day, that it is a different thing teaching children in school and teaching children in church service. It consists of the same principles but different environments, patterns of teaching even the timetable. The church uses an order of service instead of class timetable and many more differences. However, I was determined to teach that day, my fears not withstanding. Suddenly, the leader of the children's teachers asked me to go to teen's church as a new teacher to observe for that day. So while the teacher was teaching I looked, listened and learned with a sense of humility.

The next Sunday was my test, my first day as a teacher, and this experience was memorable to me. Will my fear be defeated today by my passion and faith? This was the question I asked myself that beautiful Sunday morning. As the leader was assigning teachers to the classes she said, "Uncle Lawrence, you will be in toddler's class." Honestly, I thought this wouldn't be too difficult a task as my first assignment, after all these are only babies. But little did I know that most teachers didn't like teaching this class. Either the teacher didn't understand the toddlers or the toddlers didn't want to understand. With great anticipation I walked into the class. It was not funny to see me walk into that class that beautiful Sunday morning. There was incredible noise everywhere and from everyone, as the parents were dropping the toddlers off while they themselves went to attend service in the adult church.

I thought where do I start? What do I do now? I stood in front of them wondering what to do and eventually a young teenager walked up to me and whispered in my ear, "Sir, ask one of them to take the opening prayer." As if she could read my mind, I perceived in my spirit that the she was sent from God to be my guiding helper that day. All the same I quickly asked myself, what in God's name does she mean? Can they pray? What kind of prayer will they pray? Will the prayers make sense to heaven? Later I realized that it is not the words they prayed but that they prayed. This is what matters to God, and as much as they usually end it within Jesus name, Amen! The angels carried it up to God. Answers to these prayers came sometimes sooner than from an adult's fervent spiritual prayer. I respected this young teen named Sarah. I picked a babe and told her, "Pray for us." Let me confess, the only words I heard were our Savior's name 'Jesus'. Anyway, we started as Sarah told me everything to do. Then we moved from opening prayer to praise and worship. The sequence followed as we all ended up on the floor where I sang with them, shouted with them, danced with them, and we all held hands, rolled together on the floor and I even carried them on my back.

Many, many times they went out to wee, and I had no option but fixed them on a queue to the rest room. I had my fill on that first day as a children's teacher in church. With toddlers the Word of God I shared that Sunday was a little here, a little there. Young Sarah stayed with me throughout the toddler's class for that service. I had asked her not to leave because we run two services. However, she later went to the teen's church for the second service as soon as it started. I was humble enough to allow young Sarah to teach me what to do in the first session. I heartily applied this teaching in the second session. That day I felt my joy being doubled. Oh! What joy I had been missing as a Christian. Both the playing and the teaching were great fun. I was so focused on teaching these little ones about God that I never noticed that the head teacher was in my class. Surprise!

We met the following Saturday for Sunday school preview with the head teacher asking the other teachers and assistants what they wanted to teach in respect to the service they will attend. They all picked their classes but to me she said, "Lawrence I want you in the toddler class again, you were excellent with them last Sunday, please let me have you there again." I was surprised by her request in front of the others. The toddler church became my regular group until one Sunday when I was asked to teach the teenagers, as there was no teacher in their church. When my national assignment was completed and I was leaving them, they wanted me to stay and settle down in their town. Although this was a good position I knew, God was not in it, nor was this what He wanted for me at that time.

The leadership from the children's ministry gave me a departing present—a book by A.W.Tozer titled *God's Pursuit for Man*. This book continues to bless my life by great measure. I want you to know that my first day as a teacher was a memorable experience that gave me incredible memories with the help of young Sarah.

If I could succeed with no experience you too can. So you have no excuse. If you are considering when to begin as Sunday school teacher well there is no time like the present. Enough with procrastination, Jesus needs you now to win the little ones for his kingdom, and if Jesus tarries, you will live to see them producing fruit in their lives and the lives of others. These little ones must not be lost to Hell while you are here. Much help is needed on this campaign of saving the little ones for Jesus around the world.

ABOUT THE AUTHOR

The Author LAWRENCE E. MUKORO is a pastor, educator and author. Presently, he is the founder and pastor of Millennium Christian Church, Nigeria. Pastor Lawrence teaches God's word in a dynamic way that helps believers to discover the truth that empowers them to grow in faith and live their new life in the fullness of Christ. One of his greatest passions is to see every believer grow into the fullness of Christ, and he believes this is possible. He is a man on a mission to remove the shame and reproach off the African people by reaching them with the gospel of Christ.

Before stepping into full-time ministry, he had served seven years as an active children's teacher in four different local assemblies of *Living Faith Church*, Nigeria, which is presided by Bishop David O. Oyedepo. His love for children and young people is central to his ministry, and this is what led him and his wife, Lily to found Millennium Christian School, a Christ centered Nursery and Primary School where educating the total child is the goal. The couple also serves as educators in the school. Lawrence and Lily Mukoro live in Delta, Nigeria with their daughter Sherrill. **<u>10 Effective Ways to Children's Ministry</u>** is his debut book.

ABOUT THE BOOK

<u>*10 Effective Ways to Children's Ministry*</u> details ten ways to easily teach Biblical truths and principles to children. Whether, you're actively leading children's ministry, serving as a teacher, or a daycare worker, a parent of a child, or simply have a passion to help children, this book will reveal to you new strategies to apply proven grace filled principles to the lives of the children you serve.

The "Future Church" is dependent upon our leadership today being scripturally accurate to guide children during these difficult days. Pastor Lawrence has a decade of service working in Children's ministry in Nigeria and is passionate about raising up the Future Church. In addition to his positions in church leadership, pastor Lawrence and his wife, Lily, began a Christian School where they serve as educators together. Pastor Lawrence and Lily have created a Christ centered community that educate and empowers young people to lead their nation in a positive and godly direction.

Through scriptures and personal experiences, Pastor Lawrence discovered simple ways to effectively minister to children by partnering with the dynamos power of the Holy Spirit. Now he reveals these secrets with you in his debut book <u>***10 Effective Ways to Children's Ministry***</u>.

www.ingramcontent.com/pod-product-compliance
Lightning Source LLC
Chambersburg PA
CBHW050439010526
44118CB00013B/1597